Meet an Eel

Written by Ibby Alcraft
Illustrated by Ángeles Peinador

Collins

a cool rock pool

toads in a tank

a cool rock pool

toads in a tank

sharks with sharp teeth

fish dart off

sharks with sharp teeth

fish dart off

a boat in the weeds

a long thick eel

a boat in the weeds

a long thick eel

Review: After reading

Use your assessment from hearing the children read to choose any GPCs, words or tricky words that need additional practice.

Read 1: Decoding
- Use grapheme cards to make any words you need to practise. Model reading those words, using teacher-led blending. Remove the scaffolds as the children become more confident.
- Ask the children to follow as you read the whole book, demonstrating fluency and prosody.
- For each of the following words, ask the children to point to the digraphs (the two letters that make one sound). Then ask them to read the words.

    toads (*oa*)   **sharks** (*sh, ar*)   **pool** (*oo*)   **sharp** (*sh, ar*)   **boat** (*oa*)

Read 2: Vocabulary
- Look back through the book and discuss the pictures. Encourage the children to talk about details that stand out for them. Use a dialogic talk model to expand on their ideas and recast them in full sentences as naturally as possible.
- Work together to expand vocabulary by naming objects in the pictures that children do not know.
- On page 7, discuss the meaning of **dart**. Point to the fish. Say: Some fish can move very quickly. They dart through the water with quick, sudden movements. Discuss other animals that might dart in water. (e.g. *dolphins, seals*)

Read 3: Comprehension
- Reread pages 6 and 7. Ask the children what they know about sharks and to describe any sharks in stories they have read. Ask: Would you dart off like the fish? Why? Why not?
- Tell the children that this book is about a visit to an aquarium. Most of the animals in the book are underwater except the toads. Talk about any experiences of visiting an aquarium or seeing fish in tanks.
- Turn to pages 14 and 15. Model using the pictures as prompts to describe the aquarium. Encourage the children to have a go themselves. Use questions for support, such as: What did the children see first? (*a rock pool*) What did the sharks have? (*sharp teeth*) What was the boat in? (*weeds*)